L.S. LOWRY

Damian Harvey

Illustrated by Yuliya Somina

W

FR.......ATTS

Contents

CHAPTER 1
Growing Up

Laurence Stephen Lowry was born
in Manchester, England, on the
1st November, 1887. It was the year
of Queen Victoria's Golden Jubilee
and everyone was celebrating. Well,
nearly everyone…

Laurence's mum, Elizabeth Lowry, wasn't celebrating at all. She'd been hoping for a pretty baby girl, not a big, clumsy boy like 'Laurie'.

Laurie's father, Robert, worked as an office assistant. His mum, Elizabeth, was a gifted pianist and played the church organ at Bennett Street Sunday School.

While she played, Laurie stood close by. He was very shy and stayed away from the other people.

Laurie had no brothers or sisters and he could never invite friends to the house because his mother often felt unwell.

Instead, she would take him to her sister's house, where he played with his cousins and their dolls.

During the holidays, Laurie's mother would take him to Lytham-St-Annes in Lancashire or Rhyl in North Wales. She liked to sit on the beach and watch the yachts out at sea.

When they got home, Laurie sat and drew pictures of yachts and people building sandcastles on the beach.

The Lowry family didn't have a lot of money but Elizabeth was determined to make her family appear successful. She persuaded her husband to get a house in Victoria Park – a nice part of Manchester where wealthier people lived.

They even paid a maid to clean
and to help look after Elizabeth
when she wasn't feeling well.

Laurie was sent to a private school, not the ordinary school that his cousins went to. Elizabeth wanted him to do well and get a good job, but Laurie hated it. Some of the other children teased him, and so did some of the teachers.

Laurie hated doing homework too. He wanted to spend his time drawing instead.

When he arrived home he would leave his homework on the table and go and talk to Lucy, their maid.

Laurie was good with numbers but he didn't do very well at school. He left when he was 15.

His mother was very disappointed. She knew her son wanted to be an artist, but she would never allow it – it wasn't a proper job!

Laurie really wanted to go to art college but he hadn't done well enough at school to get a place. His Aunt Mary suggested that he should have private lessons with a local artist called Reginald Barber.

CHAPTER 2
Starting to Sketch

When he was 16, Laurence Stephen Lowry got a job as a clerk with a firm of accountants. His mother was disappointed that, after going to a private school, he was only a clerk like his father.

Lowry still wanted to be an artist so he used some of his wages to pay for private lessons. In 1905, he started evening classes at an art college in Manchester.

His tutor was a French artist called Adolphe Valette who showed Lowry different styles of painting. Lowry learnt about ways of painting familiar landscapes. He also learnt to paint people.

Then, one Spring morning in 1909, the Lowry family were forced to move house. They needed to live somewhere cheaper so they moved to the industrial town of Pendlebury in Salford.

Elizabeth hated it. She hung net curtains at the windows so she wouldn't have to look at the terraced streets and poorer people passing by.

At first, Lowry hated it too. It was dark and drab with factory chimneys belching black, sooty smoke into the sky.

But then he started to see things differently and painted images in a loose style.

Lowry had a new job working for
the Pall Mall Property Company.
Instead of sitting behind a desk
all day, he walked the streets of
Salford and Manchester collecting
rent money.

Later, Lowry liked to tell people
how he had missed a train and
had to walk to Manchester. As he
reached the top of the station steps
he saw the Acme Mill with its row
of cottages running up to it.

He made sketches of the people
and places he saw and painted
them when he got back home.

Lowry wanted to improve his painting so he went to the Salford College of Art. His teacher, Bernard D Taylor, thought Lowry's pictures were too dark and the people were hard to see.

He encouraged Lowry to paint on a white background to make them brighter.

The chalky white background was good to paint on, and later it turned a nice creamy colour. It also meant Lowry could paint over pictures he didn't like.

The white background and his style of characters were one of the things that would help make Lowry's paintings stand out.

CHAPTER 3
Artist at Work

In 1919, three of Lowry's paintings were featured at the Manchester City Art Gallery. Then, a couple of years later, his work was displayed at the Mosley Street Show.

He didn't sell any paintings but some important people were starting to notice his work.

When the paintings were featured in the local newspaper, the editor liked them so much that he bought one for himself. Lowry gave him another 'as a souvenir'.

By 1930, Lowry was selling paintings at exhibitions. The Manchester Art Academy bought a painting called 'An Accident'. It was the first of Lowry's paintings to be bought for public display.

It seemed that things were finally
going well for Lowry the artist.

But then, in 1932, Lowry's father
died. He had worked all his life
to try and keep his wife happy by
giving her everything she wanted.
But his wages hadn't been enough.
He died owing people lots of money.

Lowry managed to pay off his
father's debts, but life at home
would never be the same again.

After Robert died, Elizabeth felt even more unwell. She spent the next seven years in bed, and Lowry had to look after her.

As soon as he came home from work, Lowry would wash and bathe his mother, then sit and read to her until she fell asleep.

Lowry had to give up his art studies but he didn't give up his painting. As soon as his mother was asleep, he escaped to his attic workroom to paint.

He painted the factories, streets and the strange and interesting people that he saw every day.

Looking after his mum and painting late at night was very tiring. One morning he looked at himself in the mirror. He hardly recognised his face – his hair was a mess and his eyes were so red.

After seeing himself in the mirror he painted a picture called 'Head of a Man With Red Eyes'. It's a painting that many people find scary to look at. Lowry said he had found it scary too.

CHAPTER 4
Art in Wartime

Not long after his father's death, two of Lowry's paintings were shown at the Royal Academy in London. His aunt couldn't wait to go and see the paintings for herself, but his mum took no interest in her son's art.

A friend called Daisy Jewell, who worked in a framing company and organised art exhibitions, was very impressed with Lowry's work. No one else was capturing scenes of normal everyday life in Britain the way he was.

She sent Lowry's paintings to exhibitions and galleries all over Great Britain. She even sent them to France.

Thanks to Daisy, Lowry got an exhibition all of his own in London. People bought his paintings and wrote about him in the newspapers. Lowry could hardly believe it. Maybe things were starting to get better.

But then two things happened...
Firstly, on 1st September 1939,
World War II started.

Then, just over a month later, Lowry's mother Elizabeth died. Lowry was 52, and no longer tied to his mother but, for the first time in his life, he couldn't paint. Inside he felt as empty as the house he lived in.

To get away from everything, Lowry went to the island of Anglesey in North Wales. He sat and gazed out at the sea. It gave him new ideas of things he could paint.

Lowry brought his paints and brushes down from the attic. Now, he could paint anywhere he wanted.

He hung paintings of his mother and father on the wall, and a self-portrait that he'd done years before. He joked to visitors that they were hung up to cover peeling wallpaper!

During the war, Lowry joined the volunteer fire watchers. At night, he stood on the rooftops and kept a lookout for fires.

Manchester was heavily bombed during the war. Lots of buildings were destroyed and hundreds of people were killed.

Coming down from the rooftops in the morning, Lowry saw all the ruin and destruction.

Returning home, he took up his brushes and painted what he had seen. In 1943, Lowry was made an official war artist.

CHAPTER 5
A Late Celebrity

After the war, Lowry's exhibition at the Lefevre Gallery in London was a huge success. His paintings sold very well. But even then he still kept his job as a rent collector!

Lowry's popularity kept on growing. Now even more people knew about Lowry and his paintings. He was becoming famous.

Being famous did not change Lowry. He didn't buy a big house or fast car. He never even learnt to drive. But having more money meant he could decorate his house with his favourite paintings by Dante Gabriel Rossetti.

Lowry wanted to help new artists whenever he could. He gave them advice and encouraged them when they needed it. But most importantly, he helped by buying their paintings.

In 1976, The Royal Academy in London displayed a huge collection of Lowry's work. It attracted over 300,000 visitors.

However, Lowry died on the 23rd February, 1976, just before the exhibition opened.

Lowry's work continues to attract great crowds. In 2013, the Tate Britain in London held a big exhibition of his work. Today, you can see lots of his paintings on the internet too.

Timeline

1887   Lowry is born on 1st November in Old Trafford, Manchester.

1905   Lowry attends evening art classes at Manchester Art College.

1910   Lowry gets a job as a rent collector and continues the job until 1952.

1919   Three of Lowry's works are shown in the Manchester City Art Gallery.

1932   Lowry's father dies. Lowry's paintings are exhibited in the Royal Academy, London.

1939   Lowry's mother dies. Lowry now devotes his life to painting.

1943 Lowry is appointed an official war artist.

1948 Lowry moves to Mottram-In-Logendale.

1976 Lowry dies on 23rd February. In September, the Royal Academy in London exhibits his work, attracting more than 300,000 visitors.

Website links

http://www.thelowry.com/ls-lowry/the-ls-lowry-collection

http://www.tate.org.uk/art/artists/ls-lowry-1533

http://www.bbc.co.uk/arts/yourpaintings/artists/laurence-stephen-lowry

First published in 2014 by
Franklin Watts
338 Euston Road
London NW1 3BH

Franklin Watts Australia
Level 17/207 Kent Street
Sydney NSW 2000

HB ISBN 978 1 4451 3307 2
PB ISBN 978 1 4451 3308 9
Library ebook ISBN 978 1 4451 3306 5
ebook ISBN 978 1 4451 3305 8

Dewey Decimal Classification Number: 759.2

Series editor: Melanie Palmer
Series designer Cathryn Gilbert

Printed in Great Britain

Franklin Watts is a division of Hachette Children's Books,
an Hachette UK company.
www.hachette.co.uk

Advisory note to parents and teachers: every effort has been made by
the Publishers to ensure that the websites are suitable for children and
that they contain no inappropriate or offensive material. However,
because of the nature of the Internet, it is impossible to guarantee that
the contents of these sites will not be altered. We strongly advise that
Internet access is supervised by a responsible adult.